If You Know Your History...

*From Dixie to Roonaldo – celebrating
125 years of Blue passion*

Everton

If You Know Your History...

From Dixie to Roonaldo – celebrating 125 years of Blue passion

SPORT MEDIA
Trinity Mirror North West

breedon **books**
PUBLISHING

First published in Great Britain in 2003 by

The Breedon Books Publishing Company Limited

Breedon House, 3 The Parker Centre,

Derby, DE21 4SZ.

ISBN 1 85983 395 0

Printed and bound by Scotprint, Haddington, Scotland

Contents

This book is dedicated to George Mahon, the visionary and founder father of Everton and the man who inspired the famous move from Anfield to Goodison in 1892.

Foreword
by Bill Kenwright

IN the late summer of 2002, I looked out across Goodison Park in the moments leading up to our first Premiership game against Tottenham Hotspur. It was the official launch of our '100 Years in the Top Flight' celebrations, and the sun was beaming down on a 50-strong collection of Everton heroes of yesteryear, drawn back to their spiritual home to remind those who DO know their history, that our club is simply incomparable in terms of pedigree and reputation.

We had become the first club in England to celebrate a centenary in top-flight football. And we quite rightly shouted it from the roof tops! Having spent those few, precious moments looking back, Evertonians were subsequently blessed with an entire season looking forward. A season when our magnificent young manager David Moyes picked up a well deserved Manager of the Year award, and when every player who pulled on a Blue shirt went on to the pitch and showed us exactly what that shirt meant to him.

Nothing, of course, ever stands still in football, and after a season when we so nearly reclaimed our position in European football, we find ourselves in another landmark year – our 125th anniversary. We Evertonians feel instinctively that these are exciting days and not simply because we have one of the most exciting young talents in world football within our midst. I somehow feel that there is little wrong in Evertonians allowing themselves to dream the dream that Young Wayne, our Manager, and everyone involved in the playing side of the football club is hopefully preparing us for.

When Dixie Dean first signed in at Goodison Park from Tranmere Rovers, everyone knew he was a remarkable young talent. Of course no one could predict that he would achieve immortality in the years that followed – but I'm pretty nigh convinced that our fans at the time knew something special was about to happen! Dixie was never slow in emphasising that he was an Evertonian from the moment he drew his first breath. The boy who aspires to greatness in our 125th season, also has blue blood running through his veins. Wayne will never hit 60 in a season (prove me wrong Wayne!), but he already sums up what this club is all about in terms of Blue pride and passion.

The opportunity to wallow – unashamedly – in nostalgia is a role that I know every Evertonian enjoys – so I'm convinced that this special anniversary *If You Know Your History* publication will constantly be in your hands as we all draw inspiration from the deeds of an army of Goodison giants.

I'm particularly pleased that my own boyhood hero, Dave Hickson, features so prominently. Just take a look at Davey in action, a supreme lesson in how to score a sensational diving header without a single hair moving

out of place in that famous blonde quiff! The Golden Vision; the dynasty of the Cat; Ball, Harvey and Kendall; Labby and Westy; the age of Latch and the second coming of Howard! The feats of an army of Everton heroes come alive on these pages.

Of course, you never know where history begins and where it ends. As I said, when Dixie made his Everton debut, at Arsenal on 21 March,1925, who could have predicted that this would be the start of remarkable golden age? When a young man named Ted Sagar took up his position between the posts for the first time on 18 January 1930, who could have guessed that this ultimate marathon man would still be pulling on that same jersey an astonishing 24 years later? The 'who would have thoughts' could go on and on. Such is football. A very special game. Such is Everton – a very special club.

From one Evertonian to another, can I simply say enjoy this official book, and never forget how important you are to Everton FC. A football club is nothing without its fans – and I believe we are lucky in that we have the best in the business!

Nil Satis...

Foreword
by David Moyes

FOOTBALL clubs are about many things. My challenge, as the latest in a long line of proud managers, is to think about today and plan positively for tomorrow.

However, it is impossible to ignore what has gone before, simply because Everton Football Club has such a rich and outstanding history. I'm learning fast, inspired by fans who love their Goodison heroes.

Since joining the Blues I am pleased to say that I have had the opportunity to meet many of those legends. Dozens turned up to a glittering event at St. George's Hall as we celebrated a unique achievement in the English game, becoming the first club to complete 100 seasons of top-flight football.

As I watched those former players mixing with the fans and revelling in their Everton memories, it confirmed in my mind what a special club this is.

It was a moving experience to see men like Alex Young, Alan Ball, Howard Kendall, Colin Harvey, Brian Labone, Andy Gray, Graeme Sharp, Dave Hickson and many more treated with incredible respect by fans who clearly want our club to move forward, but who will never forget the achievements of the past.

Nights like that make me all the more determined to work tirelessly to try and bring the Blues back to the forefront of English football. This is a club that deserves to be up there with the best. Tremendously high standards have been set on the back of nine League Championships and five FA Cup successes.

The club also put its stamp on Europe in the mid-Eighties when the Cup-winners' Cup was won under Howard. It is no wonder that one of the most widely heard songs at Goodison is *If You Know Your History* and it is fitting that this brand new official book to mark our 125th anniversary goes under that banner.

I am proud to be Everton manager and I'm looking forward to the challenge that lies ahead as we remember the heroes of the past while striving to achieve success in our own right.

Sheer elation as Wayne Rooney is congratulated after scoring against Aston Villa.

Catch me if you can. Wayne Rooney leaves his Arsenal marker trailing in his wake as he powers forward on another attack.

David Moyes gives goalscorer Wayne Rooney a congratulatory hug as the final whistle sounds on Everton's first win at Elland Road in 51 years, in November 2002, thanks to the youngster's stunning second half strike. The Blues won 1-0.

Everton's 'Player of the Year' in 2002-03, Tomasz Radzinski, celebrates another crucial goal with partner Kevin Campbell.

These images highlight the new mood of Evertonians. The David Moyes' Revolution has put a spring into the step of the Goodison faithful. Here the fans salute the team and pack Goodison Road before another big game. One youngster gets a unique view of his hero Wayne Rooney over a barrier at the Players' Entrance as the team bus arrives. Inside the ground it's celebration time as the fans revel in another moment of Goodison ecstasy.

Where It All Began

One of the earliest team photos, here the squad of 1889-90 gather together to be snapped after finishing a more than respectable second in the Football League that year. Twelve months later Everton were crowned Champions of the Football League for the first time. This photograph was taken on the former bowling green behind the Sandon Hotel, now a car park.

Recognise this? This picture takes us back to 1905 and how Goodison Park looked in the days of Sandy Young, Harold Hardman and Jack Sharp.

Jack Taylor was one of the great Everton stars around the turn of the last century, a man who could play in almost any position. Outside-right in the Blues' team for the 1897 FA Cup Final, Taylor was the only member of that side to appear for Everton in the 1906 Final, when he turned out at centre-half. Taylor's career came to an end after a freak accident when a fierce shot hit him in the throat and caused severe damage to his larynx. He bowed out in 1910, after 456 League and FA Cup appearances and 80 goals for the Blues.

It's hard to believe but this is how Everton fans made their way to the Crystal Palace for the FA Cup Final in 1906. And you think economy class train travel is bad. There's not a personal DVD player to be seen amongst the convoy of horse-drawn carriages as they make their way through Kingsway, London. It was all worth it though, as the Blues beat Newcastle 1-0 to claim the famous trophy for the first time.

Everton on the attack during the 1906 FA Cup Final against Newcastle United at the Crystal Palace. Note the Newcastle goalkeeper has no distinguishing jersey. Everton's Alex 'Sandy' Young scored the only goal of the game 13 minutes from time, after having had an earlier effort ruled offside.

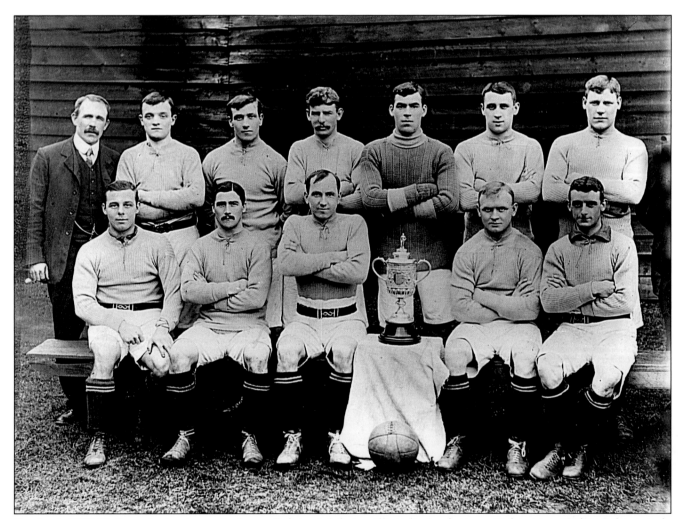

Everton's 1906 FA Cup-winning team. Back row (left to right): Joe Elliott (trainer), Harry Makepeace, Walter Balmer, Jack Taylor, Billy Scott, Jack Crelley, Walter Abbott. Front row: Jack Sharp, Hugh Bolton, Alex Young, Jimmy Settle, Harold Hardman.

… and having won the Cup it was time to celebrate. As a traditional celebratory team photo it doesn't bear much resemblance to the jubilant scenes of later years when players were a bit more partial to letting their hair down in public. Maybe they just hid it well… behind the moustaches.

Everton in 1914-15, champions of the Football League. Back row (left to right): Tom Fleetwood, Alan Grenyer, Thompson, Jimmy Galt, Tom Fern, John Maconnachie, Harry Makepeace. Front row: Sam Chedgzoy, Billy Kersopp, Bobby Parker, Joe Clennell, James Roberts.

The Dixie Dean Era

Dixie Dean was scoring goals for Tranmere Rovers when he caught Everton's eye and moved across the Mersey in 1925. His scoring record is nothing short of phenomenal: 377 goals in 431 League and FA Cup games for the Blues; 60 goals in only 39 League games in one season alone. It was fitting that when he died, it was at his beloved Goodison, minutes after the final whistle of a Merseyside derby in March 1980.

Cigarettes in hand, the victorious Championship-winning squad of 1928 appear pretty laid-back about what they have achieved. Posing with the trophy at Goodison Park, half of them can't even manage a smile. Mind you, it had been a long, hard season. It's Dixie Dean, he of the record-breaking 60 goals that year, that has the broadest grin of the lot.

Hands on hips, standing proudly on the Goodison pitch with the Gwladys Street terraces behind him, Dixie Dean cuts a confident figure, as well he might. The great man was already an Everton super hero at this stage and going on to achieve legendary status.

Dixie takes to the field and an army of Evertonians raise the roof. Our immortal captain was not just idolised on Merseyside. He was a super hero wherever he played.

The greatest honour that can be bestowed upon a player is to captain their side. Dixie Dean was a proud Everton skipper, a real leader of men. The sight of him coming out at the head of the pack inspired teammates and supporters alike.

Dixie's record-breaking 60th goal at the Park End. The quality of this picture is not the greatest but for historical significance, it can't be surpassed. Everybody has heard about Dean's record-breaking goal tally – and here's the famous strike number 60, coming against Arsenal in 1928.

The first Everton number-nine to play for England was Dixie Dean, and here he is seen in action for his country testing the reaction of Spanish 'keeper Zamora. The Spaniard is quick to gather though as Dean rushes in during the international at Highbury in December 1931

A split-second too late and the moment is lost. Even the great Dixie Dean would subscribe to that theory. "The secret of heading is to catch it on your forehead," he said. "If you get it on the top of your head it will knock you daft in no time. I was not as tall as many of the centre-halves I played against, but I never had any difficulty beating them in the air. It wasn't a case of leaping higher than they could. It was just a matter of going up at the right time." This picture sums up Dean's power and timing perfectly.

The 1929-30 season was a rare blip in the story of Everton Football Club – but it's all part of history. They were relegated from the top flight. This team lost 5-2 at Villa Park in October. Back row (left to right): Andy Kennedy (12th man), Tom Robson, Warney Cresswell, Arthur Davies, Tommy White, Tom Griffiths, Harry Cook (trainer). Front row: Ted Critchley, Tony Weldon, Monty Wilkinson, George Martin, Jimmy Stein, Jack O'Donnell.

Coming to terms with life in a lower division were Dixie Dean and Co. back in the early Thirties. This shot shows the striker and his teammates stepping out near Goodison ahead of the 1930-31 season, Everton's first ever in Division Two. Pictured with Dean (from left) are George Martin, Tommy White, Billy Coggins and Tom Griffiths. Eight months later they were to find themselves back in the top flight.

Champions of Division Two in 1930-31 – and champions of the top flight 12 months later. Everton in 1931-32, the season they lifted their fourth Football League title. Back row (left to right): Harry Cook (trainer), Archie Clark, Ben Williams, Ted Sagar, Charlie Gee, Warney Cresswell, Cliff Britton. Front row: Ted Critchley, Tommy White, Dixie Dean, Tommy Johnson, Jimmy Stein, Jock Thomson.

Ben Williams skippered Everton to promotion in 1930-31. Signed from Swansea Town in 1929, he formed a brilliant full-back partnership with Warney Cresswell and won international recognition, playing ten times for Wales. On Christmas Eve 1933 Williams was injured in the 5-1 Goodison win over Wolves and subsequently underwent a cartilage operation. He never fully recovered and was transferred to Newport County after 139 games in the Blues' first team.

Manchester City are under the cosh as Everton pile on the pressure in the 1933 FA Cup Final at Wembley. For the first time players were numbered 1-22, starting with the Blues' goalkeeper Ted Sagar. Number 19 for City is Matt Busby.

Everton take the lead in the 1933 Cup Final after City goalkeeper Len Langford dropped the ball and Jimmy Stein sidefooted it home.

The Duchess of York hands over the FA Cup to the winning captain Dixie Dean following the Blues' 3-0 win over Manchester City at Wembley in 1933. Clearly the Duchess, destined to become Queen, was impressed with our goalscoring hero. The future King George VI studies Dean with a fixed gaze.

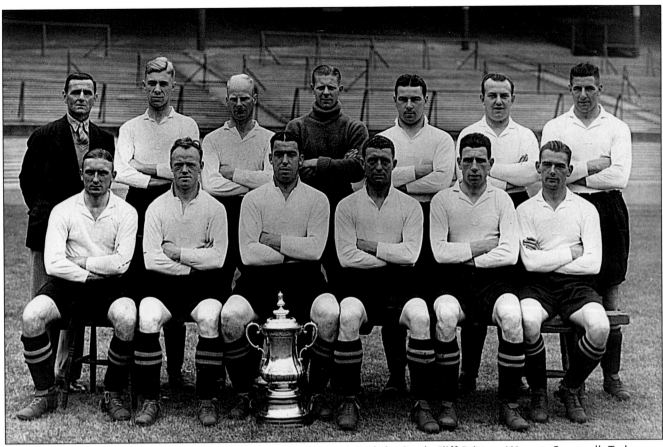

Everton with the FA Cup in 1933. Back row (left to right): Harry Cook (trainer), Cliff Britton, Warney Cresswell, Ted Sagar, Billy Cook, Tommy White, Jock Thomson. Front row: Albert Geldard, Jimmy Dunn, Dixie Dean, Tommy Johnston, Jimmy Stein, Ted Critchley.

Dixie Dean leads his teammates in celebration as they show off the silverware to the residents of Liverpool's Scotland Road.

Everton's Joe Mercer (left) and Cliff Britton enjoyed glory days at Goodison in the Thirties. Mercer started as a junior with Everton in 1932 and won a regular place three years later. He became England's left-half and made nearly 200 peacetime appearances for Everton.

Britton arrived from Bristol Rovers in 1930 and by the outbreak of war had appeared in almost 250 senior games for the Blues. With Mercer and Wolves' Stan Cullis, Britton was a member of an outstanding England middle line during the war.

(Left) Tommy Lawton scored 34 goals in 38 League games as Everton won the League title in 1938-39. He cost Everton £6,500 in March 1937 when he signed from Burnley, for whom he had scored a hat-trick on his League debut as a 17-year-old. By the time the Football League was suspended upon the outbreak of war in 1939, Lawton had scored 70 goals in only 95 games for the Blues.

Everton, Football League champions in 1938-39. Back row (left to right): Tommy Lawton, Tommy G. Jones, Ted Sagar, Harry Cook (trainer), Joe Mercer, Norman Greenhalgh. Front row: Billy Cook, Torry Gillick, Stan Bentham, Jock Thomson, Alex Stevenson, Wally Boyes. The young mascot is J. Shannon.

In September 1938 Everton won 2-1 at Highbury to underline their early challenge for the League Championship. In the 14th minute Tommy Lawton slid the ball to Alex Stevenson who (above) hammered his shot past Arsenal goalkeeper George Swindin and into the net. Everton won again the following week, 5-1 at home to Portsmouth, to make it six wins out of six from the start of the season.

Everton's Scotland international winger Torry Gillick braces himself for a lunging tackle from Arsenal's Bryn Jones.

The Post-War Years

A bumper crowd of 78,299 packs into Goodison Park for the Merseyside derby in September 1948. Everton skipper Alex Stevenson and Liverpool's Jackie Balmer step out in front of the club's biggest ever home attendance. The on-the-field honours were shared that day as Jock Dodds late penalty cancelled out Fagan's second-half opener.

Everton boasted a fine Irish contingent back in the Fifties with Republic of Ireland internationals Peter Farrell, Jimmy O'Neill and Tommy Eglington all having etched their name into Goodison folklore. Eglington didn't manage to score on this occasion in March 1950 but he tested the reflexes of Liverpool goalkeeper Cyril Sidlow as the packed terraces look on. A crowd of 72,000 were at Maine Road for this all-Merseyside FA Cup semi-final.

Dave Hickson may have played for all three Merseyside clubs but his heart lies firmly at Goodison. Hickson was a super hero in the Fifties and continues to work for the club these days as a valued ambassador. This highly unusual worm's-eye view captures Dave's shooting power in the 3-1 win over Birmingham City in October, 1958. Note the towering floodlights, a giant pylon dominating each corner of Goodison.

Everton pictured in 1960. Back row (left to right): George Sharples, Alex Parker, Brian Labone, Albert Dunlop, Jimmy Gabriel, Mick Meagan, John Bramwell. Front row: Micky Lill, Bobby Collins, Jimmy Harris, Roy Vernon, Tommy Ring.

The Swinging Sixties

When Everton hammered Chelsea 6-1 at Goodison in March 1960, new signing Tommy Ring scored twice. His was a short stay at Goodison, however. The former Clyde and Scotland outside-left was on his way to Barnsley in November 1961, after scoring six goals in his 27 League games for the Blues.

A heavy fall of snow was not enough to call a halt to proceedings at Bellefield in this training picture from 1961. Jumping as if their lives depended on winning the ball are (from left) Brian Harris, Jimmy Gabriel and Brian Labone.

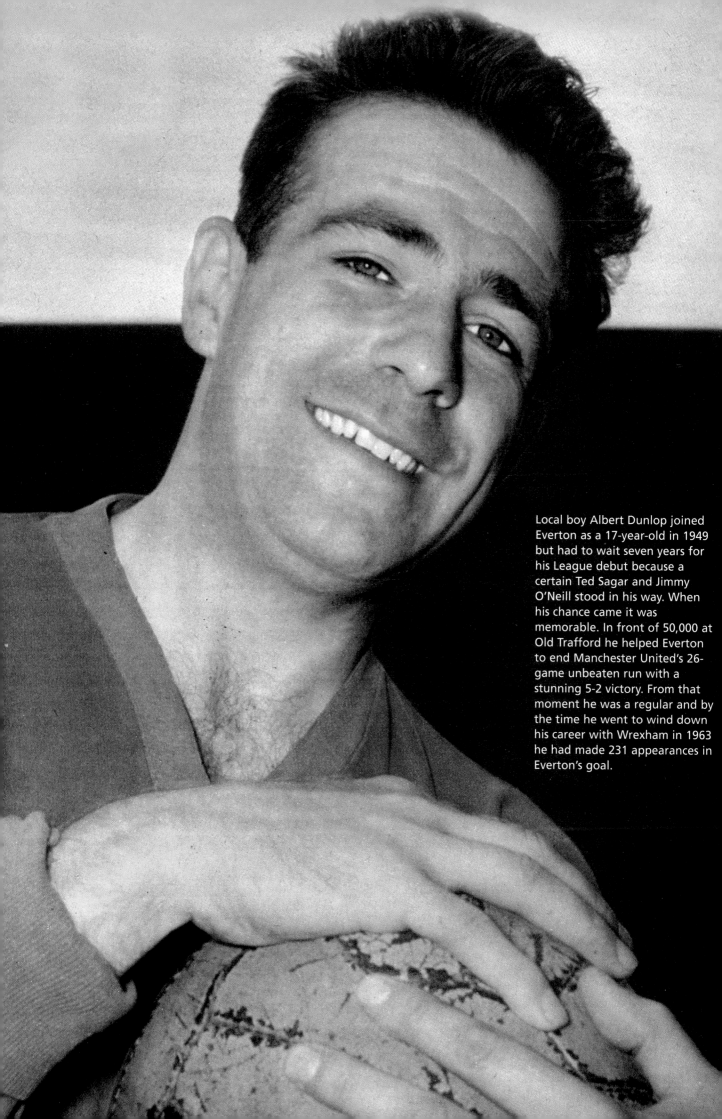

Local boy Albert Dunlop joined Everton as a 17-year-old in 1949 but had to wait seven years for his League debut because a certain Ted Sagar and Jimmy O'Neill stood in his way. When his chance came it was memorable. In front of 50,000 at Old Trafford he helped Everton to end Manchester United's 26-game unbeaten run with a stunning 5-2 victory. From that moment he was a regular and by the time he went to wind down his career with Wrexham in 1963 he had made 231 appearances in Everton's goal.

Jimmy Gabriel made one substitute appearance for the Blues – and started 300 other games. Thirty-six goals complete the statistics but do not tell the full story. He came from Dundee for £30,000 in 1960, stayed until 1967 and was a major player in the 1962-63 Championship side and the 1966 FA Cup Final victory. A powerhouse midfielder, he returned to Goodison to work on the managerial teams of Colin Harvey and Howard Kendall.

April 1963 and a rare picture of Tony Kay in action. Here he gets the boot in to beat Birmingham City's right-back Brian Rushton before sending over a cross from which Roy Vernon scores the only goal of the game at St Andrew's. His Goodison career was to come to an end the following year when he was found guilty of match-fixing, a charge relating to his day's with Sheffield Wednesday.

It was the year The Beatles phenomenon got into full swing but the explosion of the Fab Four wasn't the only big thing to happen on Merseyside in 1963. Crowds gathered for the Aintree races and three familiar faces could be spotted amongst them. George Thomson is the man on the left studying the action while Roy Vernon is the unmistakeable figure in the centre. The man on the right is, of course, the supremely talented Tony Kay.

A young fan is restrained by a nearby constable as he tries to invade the pitch at the end of the Blues' final game of the season at home to Fulham. He had every right to be happy that day in 1963 as a Roy Vernon hat-trick and an Alex Scott goal sealed a 4-1 win and the League title in front of a 60,000 strong crowd.

Alcohol? In a football stand? Yes, and well deserved it was too on this occasion. High in the Main Stand, Harry Catterick and the victorious team of '63 treat themselves to a glass or two of champagne after clinching the League title for the first time in 24 years. Tony Kay, standing next to 'The Catt', opts for a celebratory cigar instead. Also pictured are Jimmy Gabriel, Derek Temple, Albert Dunlop, Brian Labone, Alex Parker, Alex Scott and Alex Young.

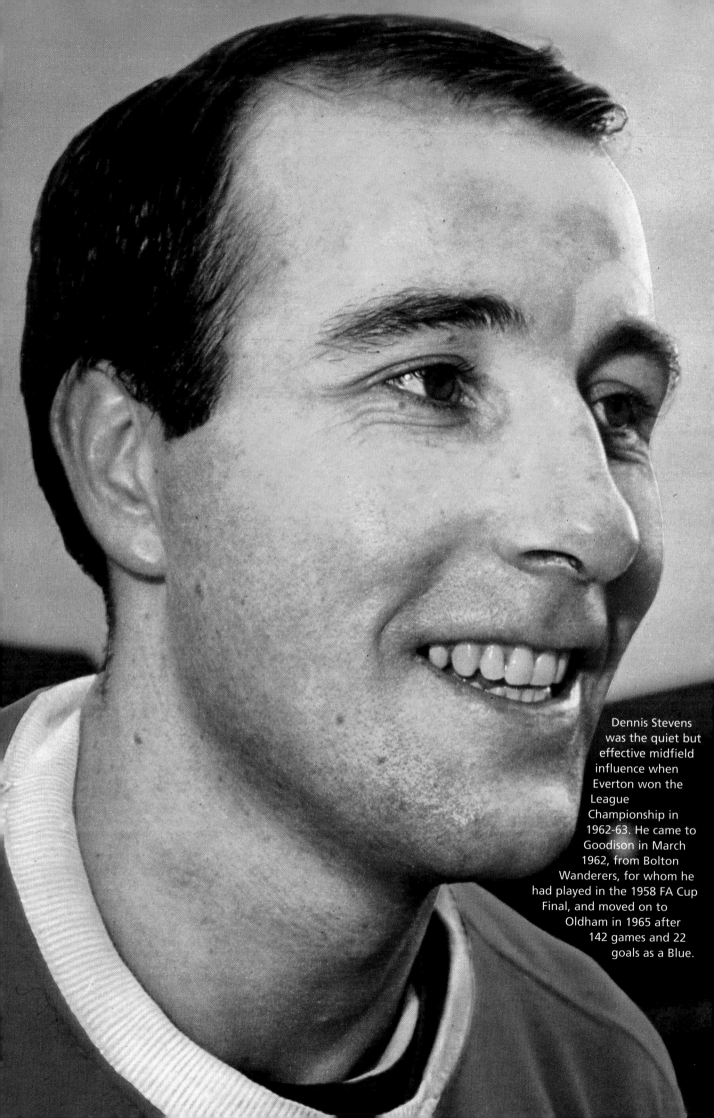

Dennis Stevens was the quiet but effective midfield influence when Everton won the League Championship in 1962-63. He came to Goodison in March 1962, from Bolton Wanderers, for whom he had played in the 1958 FA Cup Final, and moved on to Oldham in 1965 after 142 games and 22 goals as a Blue.

Alex Parker and Tony Kay, two key figures in Everton's 1962-63 Championship-winning team, share a joke at Goodison. Parker was a classic full-back who joined the Blues from Falkirk in 1958. He won 15 caps for Scotland and by the time he moved to Southport in 1965 had appeared in 219 games for Everton.

Tony Kay was a brilliant midfielder who joined the Blues from Sheffield Wednesday in 1962 for £55,000, then a British record for a wing-half. Everton suffered for his misdemeanor as a Wednesday player. Alas, he fell from grace in spectacular fashion, caught up in the sensational bribes scandal that engulfed the game in the mid-Sixties.

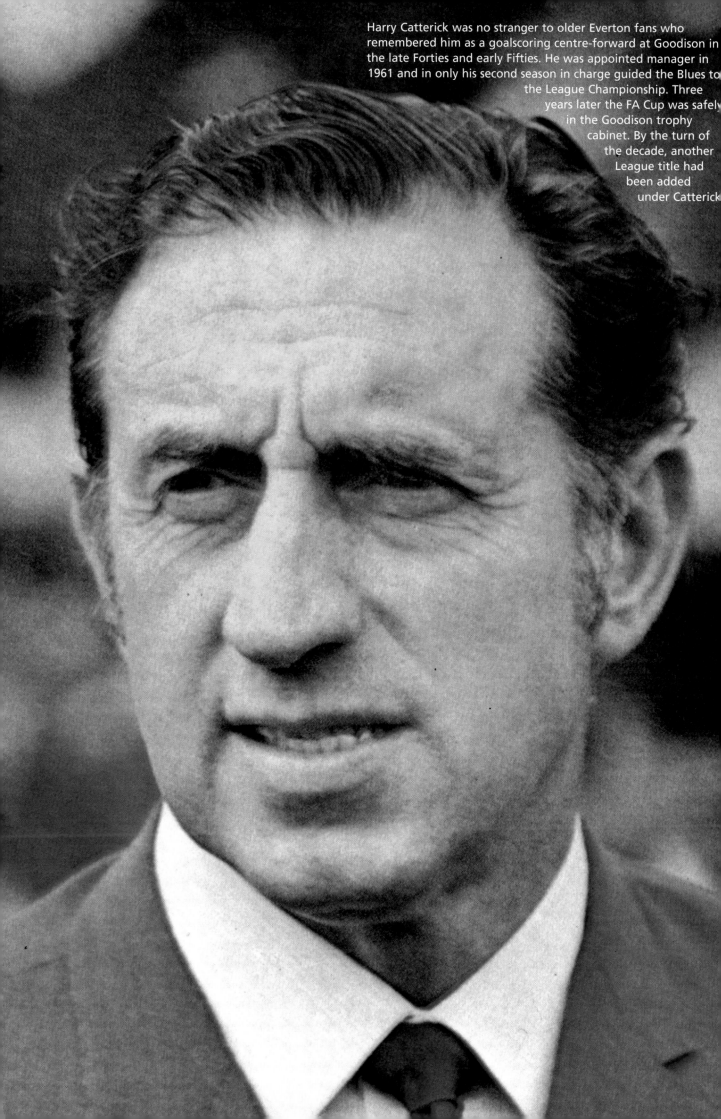

Harry Catterick was no stranger to older Everton fans who remembered him as a goalscoring centre-forward at Goodison in the late Forties and early Fifties. He was appointed manager in 1961 and in only his second season in charge guided the Blues to the League Championship. Three years later the FA Cup was safely in the Goodison trophy cabinet. By the turn of the decade, another League title had been added under Catterick

Championship celebrations spill on to the pitch in 1963 as a clutch of victorious players are chased by a lady in a tartan skirt while a photographer rushes to get his camera sorted out in time to snap the action.

It might be hard for some fans to believe, but back in the Sixties, Everton were known as 'The Mersey Millionaires' and as a result we paid top whack for a certain Fred Pickering. The Blackburn striker arrived at Goodison for a then considerable fee of £85,000, and as a result expectations were understandably high. He did not disappoint and opened his Everton account in some style, with a hat-trick against Nottingham Forest in the Blues' 6-1 rout on March 14, 1964. You could be forgiven for thinking that Roy Vernon (left) is the man on target. The real goalscorer – Pickering – is, in fact, out of shot but the photo nevertheless captures the mood of Goodison vividly during that decade.

The decision to play 16-year-old Joe Royle at Blackpool in January 1966, instead of the revered Alex Young, hadn't gone down well in some quarters. It was no reflection on Royle himself, far from it. It was a reaction to the ousting of the Golden Vision. The feelings of one Young fan are made clear towards the end of the 1963-64 season. His one-man protest during the home game with West Ham ended with a police escort off the field. His home-made placard made the point well – even if he did spell the Everton boss's name wrong.

51

Roy Vernon more than played his part in the Harry Catterick era and scored many an important goal in an Everton shirt. He was also lethal from the penalty spot as he demonstrates here in a spot-kick strike against Manchester United goalkeeper David Gaskell in 1963-64. The photographer was able to capture the moment perfectly from ground level behind the Goodison goal.

Gordon West was a superb athlete. This picture captures him in action against Liverpool, claiming a Peter Thompson cross.

Gordon West was Harry Catterick's first signing – a £27,000 capture from Blackpool. Within 12 months of taking over from Albert Dunlop between the sticks he'd won a Championship medal and went on to make a massive 399 appearances for the club.

The great Gordon West again seen in action in a derby game against Liverpool. As a character Westy was one of Goodison's untouchables. As a goalkeeper, he was international class and the whole country was stunned when he decided against going with England to Mexico for the 1970 World Cup for personal reasons.

No pictorial record of Everton is complete without the fans. Here we turn the clock back to the Sixties. A sea of expectant faces at Goodison, and a banner proclaiming their faith in the God of Gwladys Street, the Golden Vision.

In 1964 Everton spent £85,000 to bring Blackburn Rovers striker Fred Pickering to Goodison. He repaid them with 70 goals in only 115 games. Many considered him unlucky to miss the 1966 FA Cup Final and a year later he was on his way to Birmingham City for £50,000. Pickering had a memorable England debut, netting a hat-trick in a 10-0 win over the USA in New York.

Having picked off Bedford Town in the fourth round of the 1966 FA Cup competition, Everton welcomed Coventry to Goodison in the March of that year as they looked to progress even further. They eased into the sixth round with a 3-0 win. Fred Pickering and Derek Temple were on target that day as was the 'Golden Vision' Alex Young who is pictured here wheeling away in triumph after opening the scoring.

Funnily enough it's not the only time we've been party to a picture like this from a Merseyside derby. Tensions are always running high as local pride is at stake and in August 1966 it was no different. Alex Young is booked for a foul on Ian Callaghan, who receives attention as the debate goes on.

1966 And All That

The year was 1966 and a group of Everton fans kill time before our FA Cup Final date with Sheffield Wednesday by watching a young boxer going through his paces in London's Hyde Park. The boxer went by the name of Muhammed Ali and a couple of years earlier he had become world heavyweight champion after beating Sonny Liston. Definitely one to tell your grandchildren about…

Brylcreem-a-plenty as the coin toss gets things under way at Wembley in 1966. Everton skipper Brian Labone stoops to get a closer look as Sheffield Wednesday captain Don Megson, father of Gary, and the match officials – in impressively crisply ironed gear – look on.

Mike Trebilcock watches his shot speed goalwards towards Ron Springett and then past him as the Everton man scores the first of his two goals against Sheffield Wednesday to pull the game back to 2-1 in the 1966 FA Cup Final.

Trebilcock jumps for joy after scoring his second goal against Wednesday. Catterick's much-criticised last-minute selection of Trebilcock in preference to crowd favourite Fred Pickering appeared to have been vindicated. Mike's second goal (this is his second) drew the Blues level when they'd looked buried after going 2-0 down after just 12 minutes. The stage was set for one of the greatest Wembley fightbacks of all time.

Catch me if you can. Well they did eventually. Avid Evertonian Eddie Kavanagh is finally pinned down after running on to the pitch during the 1966 FA Cup Final. He'd made his way as far as the opposition penalty box before police caught up with him, losing his jacket via an unsuccessful rugby tackle by a chasing bobby. Here Blues' skipper Brian Labone begs the other boys in Blue not to arrest him as Kavanagh lies exhausted on the Wembley turf.

The Cup Final will go down as one of the most exciting ever to have taken place at Wembley. Sheffield Wednesday were 2-0 up but if you know your history then you'll remember Mike Trebilcock's double and the winner from this man – Derek Temple – in our amazing comeback.

Princess Margaret wore a pink number but it was all eyes on the Blues that famous day in 1966. Skipper Brian Labone is, of course, the man receiving the silverware as Gordon West looks on. Then it's the manager's turn to get his hands on the silverware, with a bit of help from Alex Young.

With the job done, the goal heroes, Mike Trebilcock and Derek Temple, share a well-deserved drink from the FA Cup.

It mightn't be the most reliable looking bus in the world but it was good enough to play temporary home to the FA Cup heroes of '66 as they undertook the traditional, celebratory open-topped journey around the streets of Liverpool to show off their well-earned bit of silverware.

Superstitions are a way of life for some players, although they don't always work. Here's one that did the trick though. Everton skipper Brian Labone lifted the FA Cup in 1966 and here, clinging for dear life to the silverware, is the Blues' lucky motto for the day – a black cat.

Everton with the FA Cup in 1966. Back row (left to right): Brian Harris, Brian Labone, Gordon West, Jimmy Gabriel, Tommy Wright, Tommy Eggleston (trainer). Front row: Alex Scott, Mike Trebilcock, Alex Young, Harry Catterick (manager), Colin Harvey, Derek Temple, Ray Wilson.

Goodison Park, 1966 and one of the game's greatest ever takes time out to re-hydrate himself. These days it's a high energy sports drink in a branded bottle that the players might be thrown when they are in need of refreshment. In the innocent days of 1966 however, a hot water bottle filled with nothing more exciting than 'corporation pop' did the job. If it was good enough for Eusebio...

Goodison Park was a local venue for the 1966 World Cup so it was fitting that the trophy made an appearance at the same stadium after England's memorable triumph. Ray Wilson was the Everton hero who paraded the cup in front of the Blues fans along with Liverpool's England striker Roger Hunt. There was a double reason for celebration that year, of course, with Wilson and Everton also FA Cup winners.

Ray Wilson was widely regarded as the
most stylish full-back in Europe when
he shared in England's 1966 World Cup
victory, only a few weeks after helping
Everton win at Wembley. He had
joined the Blues from Huddersfield in
the 1964 close season and made 153
appearances before injury ended his
top-flight career in 1968. He was
capped 63 times by England.

The Late Sixties

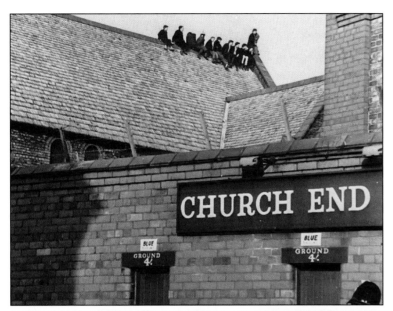

In the late Sixties and early Seventies, fans often found their way up on to the Church roof alongside the Gwladys Street terrace. Interestingly, the turnstiles declare: 'The Church End.' Who said football wasn't a religion! It is at Goodison Park.

He'd scored on his debut against Fulham and two games later Alan Ball was marking his derby debut with a valuable brace. If the little man from Blackpool didn't know about the importance of winning a Merseyside derby by then he'll have known after that. He slips the ball past Tommy Lawrence in front of the Gwladys Street for his first goal and then hammers home his second at the same end. The celebration and reaction of the crowd says it all.

Everton's first-team squad pictured before the 1968-69 season in which they finished third in the top flight and reached the FA Cup semi-finals. Back row (left to right): Roger Kenyon, Andy Rankin, Gordon West, Geoff Barnett, Joe Royle. Middle row: Wilf Dixon (trainer), John Hurst, Howard Kendall, Colin Harvey, Tommy Jackson, Alex Young, Sandy Brown. Front row: Ray Wilson, John Morrissey, Jimmy Husband, Harry Catterick (manager), Brian Labone, Alan Ball, Tommy Wright.

Sandy Brown will forever be remembered for that own-goal against Liverpool in 1969, captured here. This moment went down in Mersey soccer folklore and every own-goal after, amateur or professional, that was dubbed a 'Sandy Brown'. But the highly versatile Scot, who played in every position for Everton, did actually manage to put the ball in the enemy net as well during his time at Goodison. And here is the proof as he outleaps 'keeper Tommy Lawrence to score in the 3-1 win over the Reds in August 1966.

Any Everton goal is good but when it comes against Liverpool and two future managers are involved then it becomes special. It's February 1968, it's a League match and Howard Kendall is the man about to punch the air in delight while number-nine Joe Royle shares his excitement. Ron Yeats is the Reds' defender looking suitably aggrieved as Goodison explodes. Kendall's goal resulted in a 1-0 win for the Blues.

Two of the club's greatest servants take part in a wheelbarrow race at the Blues' Bellefield training ground in the late Sixties. Brian Labone and Gordon West clocked up 929 appearances between them during their time at the club, winning two League Championships and an FA Cup winners medal apiece. They remain the best of friends to this day.

Brian Labone began watching Everton as a schoolboy from the Goodison terraces – and ended up captaining the club to League and FA Cup glories. A stylish centre-half and the ultimate stopper, Labone clocked up 530 first-team games – he scored twice in that time – and his League tally of 451 was only 12 short of Ted Sagar's club record (and Sagar's career had lasted nine year's longer). Labone won 26 England caps and played in the 1970 Mexico World Cup. Sadly, the following year his career was ended by an Achilles' tendon injury. He won two League Championships, plus FA Cup winners' and runners-up medals with the Blues.

Heard of the *Reservoir Dogs*? Well, here's Everton's version. Boss Harry Catterick is decked out in suit and shades while his players walk with attitude towards the camera. Skipper Brian Labone, centre, leads the Sixties heroes who suggest they will stand for no messing as they prepare to board the plane for a trip abroad.

Flashback to 1967 and the first time big screens are used, on this occasion to relay the Everton-Liverpool FA Cup clash at Goodison back to Anfield. Everton won an exciting game 1-0 with an Alan Ball goal enough to set up a sixth-round match with Nottingham Forest.

Joe Royle's heading of the ball was legendary and here Liverpool's Alec Lindsay becomes the latest defender unable to get close enough to prevent the big striker from finding the back of the net. Royle may have thought this, Everton's second goal in the November Merseyside derby in 1970, would be enough to clinch the match but the Reds went on to win 3-2.

Joe Royle has been widely acknowledged as Everton's finest post-war centre-forward and his 275 games brought him 119 goals. Here he is in action against Roger Hynd of Crystal Palace.

When Everton won the Football League Championship in 1969-70, Tommy Wright played in every game. Tommy was the classic local boy made good. He joined the Goodison staff straight from school, gained an FA Cup winners' medal in 1966, won a Championship medal four years later and in the summer of 1970 played for England in the World Cup finals in Mexico. Tommy was a tough-tackling and mobile full-back who served Everton well.

In his Everton prime, Jimmy Husband was one of the most exciting wingers in the country. When the Blues won the League title in 1970, Husband was a regular member of the side. When he moved to Luton in November 1973 he had netted 55 goals in 197 games for the Blues. In 1984 he was tempted out of retirement to play for a Bedfordshire village team. Perhaps he was tempted by the name… Everton!

The Legend Of Ball, Harvey and Kendall

Alan Ball faces his teammates Tommy
Jackson, Gordon West and Howard Kendall,
after receiving a warning from the referee.
Their attitude seemed to be… "Keep cool."
Ball was booked later in the game.

A rare picture of Kendall, Harvey and Ball together in action. Here they line up in the Everton wall to face Tommy Smith's free kick in the Merseyside derby of October 1968. Alan Ball had put the Blues in front but he and the rest of the Holy Trinity couldn't prevent Smith's dead ball from finding the back of the net. The game finished 1-1.

July 1971 and it's round and round Bellefield in the warm sunshine as the Everton players, led by Wilf Dixon, return for pre-season training. Howard Kendall and Colin Harvey look ready and raring to go. Brian Labone, Gordon West and Alan Whittle head the pack.

Colin Harvey's workrate, passing and positional sense were a joy to watch. After a dramatic debut – against Inter-Milan in the San Siro Stadium in 1963 – he set about winning over Goodison's ultra-discerning faithful. They realised just what a fine player he was. He had made 383 appearances and scored 24 goals by the time he moved to Sheffield Wednesday in 1974. Harvey won an FA Cup winners' medal in 1966, a Championship medal in 1970 and was capped for England in 1971. He returned to Goodison on the coaching staff and was inspirational in the Eighties. Colin also managed the club and earned a deserved testimonial in August, 2003.

Back together again – this time as manager and his assistant, Howard Kendall and Colin Harvey plot their latest success as Everton climb back to the top in a glorious mid-Eighties spell.

Jack Charlton looks on as Colin Harvey clears Eddie Gray's cross with a powerful header during the February clash with Leeds at Goodison in 1967. Gordon West and Jimmy Gabriel watch on in the knowledge that the impending threat has been dealt with.

Colin Harvey is out of shot as the ball soars past the West Brom 'keeper John Osborne from 25 yards out to clinch the League title in April 1970. It's the Blues' second of the night and puts them out of sight in the Championship race. Harvey has left his mark if not his image on this picture.

Colin Harvey lets rip in the FA Cup semi-final with Manchester United at Burnden Park in April 1966 and (next page) leaps for joy as his powerful effort sears past United 'keeper Gregg to clinch Everton's place in the 1966 FA Cup Final. And we all know what happened next…

Alan Ball leads out the reigning champions for the 1971 Goodison derby clash with Liverpool while someone called Smith heads the opposition line-up. Look at that crowd, they can hardly contain their excitement can they? Did they know there would be no goals?

The legendary Alan Ball, Colin Harvey and Howard Kendall pictured together at a recent Everton function. How much would they be worth in the modern game as an unmatchable threesome? You wouldn't have a cheque book that was big enough!

Skipper Alan Ball leads out Everton, followed by Gordon West. One the of the greatest players ever to wear an Everton shirt, the fiery midfielder cost a British record £110,000 when he signed from Blackpool in August 1966. For the Blues he clocked up almost 250 first-team appearances and scored 78 goals. Ball arrived at Goodison with a World Cup medal in his pocket.

Goodison Life

Laugh along with those loveable Reds. Ah, didn't we just when the Kop decided to present our legendary 'keeper Gordon West with a little gift. The flamboyant Westy enjoyed a warm relationship with the Kopites, having once blown them a kiss in response to their fusillades. Their response was to present him with the now famous red handbag, a source of light relief in many a Merseyside derby with the name 'Honey West' emblazoned on it.

This outstanding picture sees Alan Ball's attempts to connect with Tommy Wright's centre beaten away by Spurs' and Republic of Ireland 'keeper Pat Jennings as Everton pile on the pressure in the final minutes of this game in January 1971. Having already scored that afternoon, Joe Royle loiters nearby looking to feed off any scraps but the Blues ended up losing the game 2-1.

It's a snap that could have been taken during World War Two but was in fact taken three decades later, in 1971, as the remainder of the Main Stand was demolished so the new structure that shores up one side of Goodison to this day could be completed.

August, 1971 and another trophy is added to the list as goals from Howard Kendall and Alan Whittle see off Chelsea in the Charity Shield. Alan Ball, Colin Harvey, Joe Royle and Co. are captured celebrating their 2-1 win over the Londoners – with mugs of tea?

Tommy Lawton, Alex Young and Dixie Dean, three of the greatest centre-forwards in the club's history, if not the English game. Their contribution to Goodison legend is such that Everton fans of every age know the names whether they've seen them play or not. This picture captures the moment the three met at a dinner in the Seventies. As individuals they were outstanding. Just how good they would have been as a trio is too much of a teasing thought.

The Barren Seventies

A toothless John Connolly jumps for joy after scoring for the Blues against Newcastle in September 1972.

A year later, December 1973, the distinctly happy looking trio of Mick Bernard, Alan Buckley and John Connolly are about to be disappointed as Mike Lyons' header against Liverpool is ruled out. Not only that, the Blues end up losing the game 1-0.

Mick Lyons was probably 'Mr Everton' to most fans of his era. Between his debut in 1970-71 and his last season in 1981-82, he played in 460 games and scored 59 goals for the Blues. Born in Croxteth, he came through the ranks. He joined the club as a striker but was switched to centre-half with great effect. Sadly. Mick won no major honours during his time at Goodison.

England international midfielder Martin Dobson set a new British transfer record when he came to Goodison from Burnley for £300,000 in August 1974. By the time he surprisingly quit Everton to return to Turf Moor in 1979, he had played in 230 games for the Blues and scored 40 goals as well as adding another England cap.

Eye on the ball, finger on the pulse, new manager Billy Bingham is pictured with Howard Kendall in 1973. Bingham took over from Harry Catterick, the man he had played under in the first half of the Blues' 1962-63 League Championship-winning side. In 1974-75 it looked as if he might deliver another title but the side eventually finished fourth.

These boots were made for running through a brick wall in the name of Everton. Battling Seventies hero Mick Lyons gets ready for action.

Despite the Championship being lifted at the start of the decade, it's fair to say the Seventies weren't especially memorable – the odd bright spark apart. Bob Latchford became a firm favourite with fans following his move from Birmingham City and cemented his popularity in 1977-78 by becoming the first English player in six years to hit 30 top flight goals in a season. This picture from the 1974-75 campaign captures the bearded hitman celebrating one of his two goals in a League match against Carlisle United. The young fan standing to his right looks suitably impressed too.

It's the start of a new campaign and the players are assembled for the traditional pre-season photo. Just for good measure, Everton opened up the gates to some young fans who were only too pleased to get a glimpse of their heroes. Hands up those old enough to have bought the classic kit?

Striker Bob Latchford needed two goals from the final game of 1977-78, against Chelsea, and netted the record and a £10,000 prize from a national newspaper. When Latchford left Goodison for Swansea in the close season of 1981 he did so as Everton's highest post-war League goalscorer with 106 from 235 games.

If you're going to take tips on how to improve your game, then you may as well listen to the best. That's what Bob Latchford did when Dixie Dean popped in for a chat at Bellefield back in 1974.

'If we sneak out now do you think they'll notice?' It's not often that you get two Everton legends of such standing together in the one place but the organisers of a sportsman's dinner at Tranmere Rovers did just that. Here the camera captures a pivotal moment as Joe Mercer bends the ear of Rovers' old boy Dixie Dean.

Martin Dobson takes one right on the nose as he clears the ball away from the impending danger of Jimmy Case during the FA Cup semi-final clash with Liverpool at Maine Road in April 1977. It was a game remembered for reasons other than the typical Merseyside derby spirit.

Martin Dobbo, oh, oh …Martin Dobbo, Martin Dobbo! Our talented Seventies midfielder relaxes on the team bus.

Peter Scott blasts in a shot at Goodison in the Seventies.

A stroll by Stanley Park Lake in the Seventies for George Telfer, Martin Dobson, David Jones and Ken McNaught. It's been many a year since a rowing boat has been seen on the lake. But then it's many a year since a posse of Everton stars have taken it on themselves to stroll in the sun in this particular green oasis.

We all know it was a goal but sadly Clive Thomas wasn't of the same opinion. Liverpool's Joey Jones looks on as Irishman Bryan Hamilton steers the ball past Ray Clemence in the semi-final of the FA Cup at Maine Road in 1977. The game was drawn and the Blues' arch-rivals went on to win the reply 3-0.

This goal did stand in that match against Liverpool in April 1977, however. Here Duncan McKenzie slots one home and there is little Terry McDermott can do about it but watch.

They'd struggle to uncover much to shout about on the pitch in the Seventies but this lot had no qualms about searching for clues off the pitch ahead of their League Cup Final clash with Aston Villa in March 1977. Duncan McKenzie, an inquisitive Bob Latchford, Martin Dobson and an even more inquisitive Bruce Rioch are pictured taking time off before the big day to play a detective game.

Bob Latchford heads straight to the Elland Road terraces after scoring in the 1980 FA Cup semi-final replay with West Ham. Sadly it proved to be a mere consolation as the Hammers went through to the Final but Latchford did have cause for celebration that year as he hit his 100th League goal at Goodison Park.

Any goal against the old enemy is worth savouring, which is why this Imre Varadi gem from 1981 is well worth a look. Ray Clemence is left in a tangle in the net as the Blues' marksman celebrates his strike from the fourth round FA Cup tie in January 1981. Everton won 2-1 with Peter Eastoe the other man on target. Evertonians were the first to the bar after the victory and the drink they ordered from the Kopite barman? You've guessed it – Varadi and Coke.

Peter Eastoe was Everton's leading scorer in 1980-81 with 19 goals in a total of 51 games. He had arrived at Goodison from QPR in 1979, in an exchange deal with Mick Walsh, and moved to West Brom in 1982, in a straight swap for Andy King.

Goalkeeper George Wood is down and in need of treatment in a derby game against Liverpool. Skipper Mike Lyons tells the referee what he thinks.

In the days before the Park End was revamped to become a hotbed once more for Evertonians, there was a spell in the Seventies and early Eighties when the area under the old stand was blocked off. Fans often stood on the resulting ledge for a better vantage point.

George Wood guarded Everton's goal in every League game for two seasons in the late Seventies. Gordon Lee signed him from Blackpool in August 1977 and he was ever-present for the next two seasons. Such consistency earned him a Scotland call-up but in August 1980, having lost his place to Martin Hodge, Wood moved to Arsenal for £150,000.

Mike Lyons would run through walls for Everton – but he'd score plenty of goals as well. For a boyhood Evertonian there is no sweeter moment than beating those from the other side of Stanley Park. So it's no surprise when the final whistle sounds that the big man looks like the cat who's got the cream as a packed Bullens Road stand celebrates behind him.

Merseyside derbies produced a lot of different emotions and tension was always bubbling near the surface. Occasionally it boiled over.

A rare picture of that great character Brian Clough and his right-hand man Peter Taylor in the Goodison Park dug-out. They brought talented teams to Merseyside during reigns at both Derby County and Nottingham Forest. While at Forest the controversial Clough called Howard Kendall 'a young pup'. The ever-humourous Howard responded immediately in his own press conference by putting a finger up to his mouth and declaring: "I'm saying nothing. I'm a Hush Puppy!"

Some rivalries never go away. Here former Liverpool captain Emlyn Hughes, often public enemy number one as far as Evertonians are concerned, finds himself on his backside as a Wolves player with Andy King standing over him, being restrained. Is that a certain Andy Gray coming in as a Wolves player to have his say?

This was quite simply the goal that signalled the beginning of the end of a long spell in the wilderness. It had been 18 years since the Goodison trophy cabinet had welcomed home a significant piece of silverware, and having lost out to Liverpool in the League Cup Final replay only seven weeks before, the desire to make sure the 1984 FA Cup Final didn't get away was plain for all to see. The prolific Scot Graeme Sharp banged home the opening goal of the game eight minutes before half-time, finding himself in space thanks to a slight deflection from a hopeful Trevor Steven ball.

You can just imagine him analysing the incident in a television studio right now and he'd no doubt argue that the goal deserved to stand – as indeed it did. Graeme Sharp had already put us in front when Andy Gray contested a high ball with 'keeper Steve Sherwood. The ball ended up in the net and the goal was given despite Watford protests. As this picture suggests, justice was done and the Cup as heading back to Everton.

Andy Gray wheels away after his
Wembley winner against Watford.

Kevin Ratcliffe joins the exclusive club of those who've had the privilege of lifting the FA Cup as he leads his
teammates up the Wembley steps following Everton's 2-0 win over Watford in 1984. Here the Duchess of Kent
congratulates 23-year-old Ratcliffe before he does the honours.

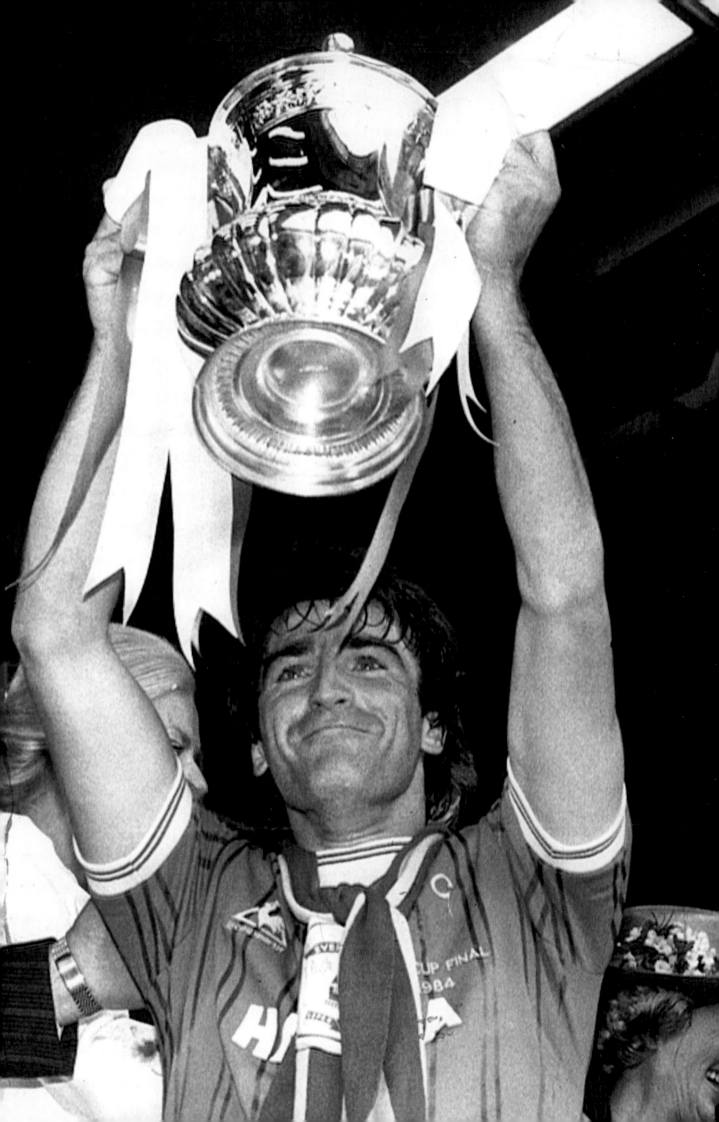

There is no hiding their delight as the squad assembles on the Wembley turf for the traditional team photo after their FA Cup win over Watford. Adrian Heath examines his winners medal more closely, and who could forget John Bailey's famous hat.

Andy Gray would stick his head where others feared to put a boot in. Remember Notts County when, as his manager Howard Kendall put it, Gray 'rotivated the ground with his nose' in the process of scoring. Here, the Scot, supposedly past it, hurls himself at the ball to net one of two goals in the Blues' 4-1 win over Sunderland during the Championship-winning season of 1984-85.

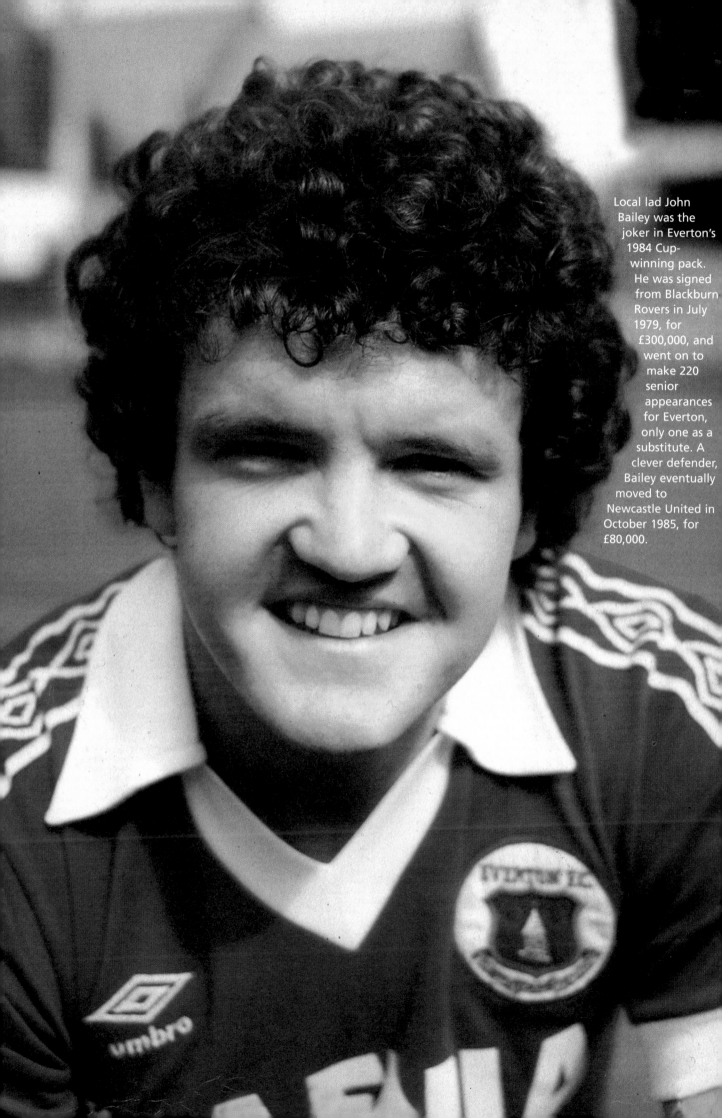

Local lad John Bailey was the joker in Everton's 1984 Cup-winning pack. He was signed from Blackburn Rovers in July 1979, for £300,000, and went on to make 220 senior appearances for Everton, only one as a substitute. A clever defender, Bailey eventually moved to Newcastle United in October 1985, for £80,000.

Almost anything to do with that magical Cup-winners' Cup semi-final clash with Bayern Munich deserves inclusion. Andy Gray's second fired us into an aggregate lead over the Germans en route to burying them and Trevor Steven's third sealed a magical win. Close your eyes and remember the feeling that words simply cannot describe.

Andy Gray leaps in the air after scoring against Bayern Munich at Goodison in the now legendary European Cup-winners' Cup semi-final in 1985.

Graeme Sharp bagged many a crucial strike in a prolific spell at Everton and judging by the celebration not many will have been sweeter than this. When you've not won the title in 15 years you want to be the one scoring the goals that help change all that. Here Sharp does the honours against QPR to install the Blues at the top once again.

It's the moment we'd all been waiting for. It had been 15 years since the League title had last resided at Goodison – but now it was back. The date is May 8, 1985, the venue Goodison Park and skipper Kevin Ratcliffe lifts the Canon League trophy to signal Everton's return to the top of the pile before the victorious squad parade the trophy in front of an ecstatic home crowd.

Graeme Sharp was virtually unknown when Gordon Lee paid £120,000 to bring him to Goodison from Dumbarton in April 1980. It was the arrival of fellow Scot Andy Gray which saw Sharp's career take a dramatic upturn. He scored the first goal in the 1984 FA Cup Final and the following season found the back of the net 30 times as the Blues won the League Championship. Scotland caps followed and when Everton were League and FA Cup runners-up in 1985-86, Sharp formed a fine partnership with Gary Lineker. Restricted by injury in the 1986-87 title-winning season, he left for Oldham for £500,000 in the 1991 close season. His Everton record was hugely impressive: 150 goals in 432 appearances.

What do you do when you've just won a League Championship at the club you once played for, and you've now managed the side to the club's first Championship in 15 years? Back in the dressing room after the crowd have gone home, Howard Kendall reflects upon the enormity of what has just happened with a glass of bubbly and a few seconds to himself. We wonder whether he was pondering the fact that just two seasons earlier people had been calling for his head. It's a funny old game.

Andy Gray fires in the opening goal in the 1985 European Cup-winners' Cup Final against Rapid Vienna. What a night it was as the Blues powered on to secure their first-ever European trophy. By then, of course, Andy's status as a Goodison legend was already secure.

This is one of those pictures that really needs no description for the vast majority of Evertonians. Rotterdam… Rapid Vienna… European Cup-winners' Cup, 1985… you know the score. Andy Gray celebrates after writing his name into Goodison folklore with the opening goal in the De Kuip Stadium on that magical night. Graeme Sharp was first on hand to start the celebrations, closely followed by Paul Bracewell.

There was no danger of Neville Southall not collecting his medal on this occasion. The hard work had been done at Goodison three weeks before when German giants Bayern Munich had been destroyed, so picking off the challenge of Rapid Vienna in Rotterdam proved a great deal more straight-forward. This was the European stage, and Everton were kings of it for the first time in their history. No wonder one of the goalscorers that night, Andy Gray, could smile, despite having the big man on his back.

Andy Gray, Peter Reid and Graeme Sharp have the Cup-winners' Cup for company as they enjoy the plane ride back from Rotterdam after the club's first-ever European success. Understandably they were in jubilant mood as they looked to claim a unique treble in the following week's FA Cup Final.

Gary Lineker and Graeme Sharp proved productive partners in 1986. New signing Lineker finished with 40 goals and went to the World Cup with England where he was the competition's leading scorer. It would lead to a shock transfer to Barcelona. Incredibly, Everton went on to win the Championship without Lineker the following season, a masterstroke from Howard Kendall who believed the Blues had altered their successful style to accommodate the striker, resulting in too much responsibility falling on his shoulders.

Opinion is split over how to view Gary Lineker's spell at Goodison. What can't be quibbled over though is his stunning 40-goal haul during his 12-month stay at the club – and this picture from the archives captures just one of them. Not since Dixie Dean had anyone come up with figures like that. Ironically it wasn't enough to earn him a Championship medal and Lineker got off to Spain.

Peter Reid salutes the fans with the League trophy as Goodison celebrates its second English title in three years, in May 1987.

Moody even on a good day. Here 'Psycho' Pat Van Den Hauwe sits in the Goodison dressing room thinking about his next victim. Pat was a fearsome character and a Championship winner for Howard Kendall.

Trevor Steven and Gary Stevens enjoy their moment with the Championship trophy. Sadly, within 12 months the latter had left for Glasgow Rangers and the lure of European football was to ensnare his right-sided partner another year on.

It's the Dave Watson celebratory salute we came to know and love over the years – and one which no doubt inspired the Alan Shearer goal celebration that we see today. On this occasion he ecstatically wheels away after claiming one of the Blues' four goals against West Ham in April 1987. Adrian Heath wasn't on the scoresheet that day but is quick to share in Watson's delight.

End Of An Era – Post-Kendall

Eleven years after they were first erected, Goodison's fences were torn down in April 1989 following the tragic events at Hillsborough when 96 Liverpool fans died. This photo captures the symbolic gesture as the city united in grief.

Stuart McCall was a tremendous purchase by Colin Harvey from Bradford, as was Tony Cottee who arrived from West Ham for a club record fee. The duo show their delight after a McCall strike at Goodison.

"I don't think Tony Cottee has had a touch yet... he might get one nowww!..." screamed BBC commentator Barry Davies as the little striker stole in with the equaliser during one of the most memorable matches Goodison has staged. On as a late substitute that night, Cottee pounced in the last minute to take the FA Cup fifth-round replay into extra-time. He was at it again not too long after, joining Graeme Sharp and Peter Beardsley on a brace of goals to take the game to a second replay. For spine-tingling value however, it's his first of the night that gets the vote. The game ended 4-4.

A legendary goalkeeper and an individual if ever there was one. This photograph summed up everything Neville Southall was about during his time as the Blues' number-one. The venue, of course, is Wembley and the occasion is the 1991 Zenith Data Systems Cup Final against Crystal Palace. While the rest of his teammates go up for a medal, Big Nev stands alone, watching from the touchline. He simply didn't want a loser's medal.

The Hillsborough disaster brought about many changes in the English game, not least the end of standing on the terraces. For the traditionalists it was hard to take, the advent of all-seater stadiums doing nothing but dampen the atmosphere. Here, in May 1991, Blues young and old stand on the Gwladys Street terraces for the final time as Everton beat Luton Town 1-0 thanks to a Tony Cottee goal.

Peter Beardsley was one of those brave enough to cross Stanley Park in the name of football and proved himself one of the Blues' most influential attackers after his move from Liverpool in the summer of 1991, scoring 19 goals in 48 games. Here he buries one from the penalty spot as Everton draw 2-2 with Middlesbrough.

Day Of Destiny

This was the moment when hope sprang eternal, as the ball leaves the boot of Barry Horne in the 'day of destiny' match against Wimbledon in 1994. Having clawed the game back to 2-1 after conceding two ground-silencing early goals, the midfielder let rip from fully 30 yards. Those in the Gwladys Street stand had the best view in the house as the ball swerved wickedly before crashing in the off the post. Sheer ecstasy.

At the end of the most amazing afternoon's in Everton history, on the final day of the 1993-94 season, Graham Stuart is mobbed by elated Blues as he runs off the pitch grasping the match ball. It could all have been so different. An hour earlier it had looked as if the Blues were going to lose their top-flight status after falling two goals behind in a must-win game with Wimbledon. But Stuart's two goals and a rare Barry Horne piledriver ensured one of the greatest comebacks of all time. Happy? Just a bit.

By Royle Appointment

It was one heck of a wedding night for Joe Royle. From the moment the whistle signalled the beginning of his first game in charge, a Merseyside derby, the points looked destined to stay at Goodison Park. This bullet header from the on-loan Duncan Ferguson got the ball rolling and Paul Rideout's subsequent effort finished the job. A magical night and the start of a five-year run of derby dominance.

In theory, Daniel Amokachi shouldn't have been on the pitch in the first place. But with the injured Paul Rideout getting treatment at the side of the pitch during the FA Cup semi-final against Tottenham at Elland Road, the popular African took it upon himself to come on in his place. Within minutes he'd found the back of the net and no sooner had he finished celebrating with Graham Stuart, he'd grabbed another. Game, set and match Everton.

One royal meets another as Everton line up ahead of their biggest game in years. Substitute Duncan Ferguson looks on as Dave Watson introduces the heir to the throne to the man already on it.

Everton had already denied the nation the final people wanted, according to many so-called experts, in trouncing fashionable Spurs at in the semi-final at Elland Road. Having got to Wembley only Manchester United stood in the way of the Blues and the biggest domestic cup in the business. It looked like the opportunity had been lost when Graham Stuart's cross cannoned off the cross bar but Paul Rideout leapt high to bury the rebound before wheeling in celebration – to the obvious relief of Stuart.

The boys of '95 with the holy grail of English football, the FA Cup. Skipper Dave Watson holds the trophy after the victory over Manchester United with Graham Stuart, Daniel Amokachi, Joe Parkinson, Anders Limpar, Gary Ablett, Matt Jackson and Barry Horne joining in the celebrations.

The FA Cup comes home in 1995 and 300,000 line the streets of Liverpool to greet it as the Blues parade their first piece of silverware since 1987.

Injury restricted the cult hero of the Nineties to just 39 minutes of Wembley action in what was billed by many as the David and Goliath FA Cup Final in 1995. The giant was slain, as we know, by a Paul Rideout header and come 5pm, blue noses were being donned by all and sundry in celebration of Everton's first piece of silverware in eight years. Duncan Ferguson risked the hard man image by joining in.

Anders Limpar brought tremendous skill down the flanks for Everton during Joe Royle's reign. Here he celebrates a goal at Goodison.

The Ukranian winger Andrei Kanchelskis had barely worn the Royal Blue shirt before he was cruelly upended by his former Manchester United teammate Lee Sharpe and consequently ruled out for six weeks with a dislocated shoulder. This picture captures the moment perfectly. Thankfully for Everton he was to recover to become the club's leading goalscorer with 16 goals in his debut season. If only he had hit the same heights in the campaigns that followed.

Andrei Kanchelskis proved an exciting buy by Joe Royle from Manchester United. However, Kanchelskis would often go for broke when a more measured team approach could have produced much brighter possibilities. In the end, he was allowed to move to Fiorentina and was never the same force again.

The Everton bench explode with delight after an Everton goal during Joe Royle's managerial reign. Here Joe celebrates with Anders Limpar.

Neville Southall, accompanied by his daughter, is applauded on to the Goodison Park pitch for his well-deserved testimonial match against Celtic in 1995.

Little did we know. Wayne Rooney lines up alongside Dave Watson as mascot in the 1996 Merseyside derby at Anfield.

Kendall Returns

Arthur Daley might have needed just the one minder but Mr Ravanelli needed a small gathering to look after him when he arrived at Goodison Park to run the rule over his prospective new home. He didn't like it. It was his loss.

Any picture of a Liverpool defender being undone in a Merseyside derby is particularly poignant. Neil Ruddock had already given the Toffees a helping hand with a timely own-goal when he was turned inside out by Danny Cadamarteri who ensured a memorable victory on a cold autumn afternoon back in 1997. Beautiful, but sadly for the dreadlocked striker it was more a one-off romance than the beginning of a long term affair.

139

It's what many of us wanted to do but only one it seems could go through with it. Unable to watch any longer as arguably the most important 90 minutes in the club's history unfolded, Goodison legend Brian Labone is alone with his thoughts as he paces up and down outside the ground as Everton fight for their Premiership life inside it.

This time the stakes were even higher. Everton's fate had been in their own hands in 1994 but when Coventry arrived at Goodison on the final day of the 1997-98 season the events at Chelsea could conspire to take them down anyway. The weather was miserable and the occasion sombre until Gareth Farrelly banged in a long-range volley after just seven minutes. Down at Stamford Bridge, where a draw for Bolton would condemn the Toffees to the drop, Chelsea were leading. With a minute to go Goodison fell quiet as Dion Dublin's header slipped through the grasp of Thomas Myhre. With news filtering through that Chelsea had gone 2-0 up, the sounding of the final whistle minutes later sparked scenes of jubilation on the bench like (almost) never before.

Those who still had the use of their body by this point ran en masse on to the Goodison turf as an intense feeling of relief swept around Goodison Park on the final whistle. Coventry fans stayed on to applaud as thousands of emotionally drained Evertonians celebrated Premiership safety. A 1-1 draw on the final day of the 1997-98 season was enough to pip Bolton in the race for Premiership safety.

Turn Of The Century

The tale goes that Kevin Campbell almost single-handedly kept us in the Premiership with nine goals in the space of just five games following his loan move from Turkish side Trabzonspor. It's a theory few would argue against. This was possibly his finest hour. West Ham arrived at Goodison hoping to cement a European spot but they were blown away as Campbell blasted a hat-trick as the Blues ran riot in a 6-0 win. Here Campbell draws back the trigger and the Hammers are about to go 5-0 down.

Kevin Campbell trains alone in the grounds of Mottram Hall Hotel in Cheshire, hoping that a permanent move from Turkish side Trabzonspor can soon be secured. Campbell scored nine goals in five games during his on-loan stint at the end of 1998-99 campaign. On the day Everton started their pre-season preparations for the next season, the striker cut a lonely figure as he kept himself in trim, waiting for an end to the protracted negotiations.

It wasn't the first time we'd seen the big man's chest stripped bare but the reason for the unveiling this time was particularly sweet. The month is April and the year 2001. Ferguson whips off his shirt and hurls it around his head after putting one past the old enemy. Sadly the Blues' went on to lose that match but this picture still burns brightly in the memory.

It's Kevin Campbell's favourite Everton goal to date and one that no doubt ranks high in many an Evertonian list. The hold that Joe Royle had established over our neighbours was as firm as ever in September 1999 and Campbell's early strike on a vibrant Monday night across the Park extended that run another game. Any victory over the Reds is sweet but when it's done on their patch... oh yes.

Most pictures we have selected capture a glorious moment in the club's history. A match-winning strike, the moment some silverware was placed in our hands or a moment typical of one of our most famous players. This awarding-winning shot doesn't fall into any of those categories but for artistic quality it is second to none as it captures David Weir, Gary Naysmith and Abel Xavier embroiled in an aerial tussle with the Aston Villa frontline.

SEASON
MEMBERSHIP
VOUCHER
NUMBER

GWLADYS ST. STAND
SEATS 1-85

29   28

The homecoming of a
legend is always
emotional. So it was
when Everton immortal Alex
Young took time out from his testimonial preparations in 2001 to
reflect on years gone by. Young was captured in pensive pose as he gazed
into the distance outside the Gwladys Street End of the ground where he made his
name. After seven seasons at the club, in 1968, the 'Golden Vision' left Merseyside behind,
heading at first for a brief spell in charge of Glentoran. His heart, however, remains at Goodison – as
this picture shows.

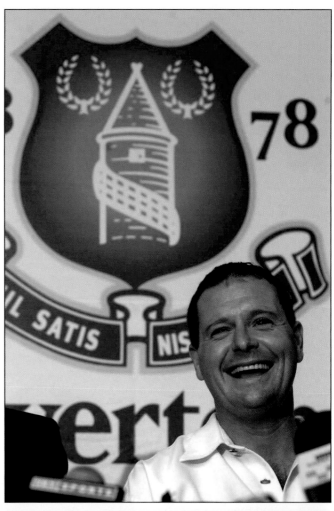

The irrepressible Paul Gascoigne is unveiled as Everton's latest signing before flying out to Italy to link up with his new teammates at their pre-season training camp.

A moment to savour at Bolton's Reebok Stadium after Paul Gascoigne buried his first League goal in nearly four years and his first goal in Everton colours. David Unsworth's reaction to his teammate's strike summed up the feelings of those around the ground as the former England midfielder proved there was life in the old dog yet. It looked to be the winning goal as well until Michael Ricketts back-heeled an injury-time equaliser.

(Left) For sheer dramatic quality, this mesmerising picture of Thomas Gravesen finds it's way into the collection. His wasn't the only goal that day as a rampant Everton side thrashed West Ham 5-0 but the Dane's mazy run and strike was the pick of the bunch and his celebration the most theatrical. And they wonder why he was nicknamed 'Mad Dog' at his former club Hamburg.

The start of something great. Following the departure of Walter Smith, David Moyes is unveiled to the nation's media just hours after accepting the offer to become Everton's new manager. There are just nine games of the season left for the former Preston man to stave off the threat of relegation.

Arrival Of The Moyessiah?

Only 27 seconds of Moyes' first game in charge had elapsed when David Unsworth's steered the ball home past Edwin Van Der Sar to put the Blues 1-0 up against Fulham. Goodison went crazy as an intense feeling of optimism swept around the ground. Unsworth wheels away to begin his goal celebration, with Duncan Ferguson in hot pursuit.

David Unsworth helps Tomasz Radzinski celebrate as the Canadian helps the Blues on their way to a third win in four games at the end of the 2001-02 season, edging them towards the Premiership safety line. Everton completed a 3-1 win over their relegation rivals Bolton, despite the sending-off of Duncan Ferguson. The Blues left the field to a standing ovation.

Three games later it was time to celebrate again as Steve Watson hit the winning goal down at Southampton to all but secure Everton's place in the top flight as the Moyes' revolution gathers pace.

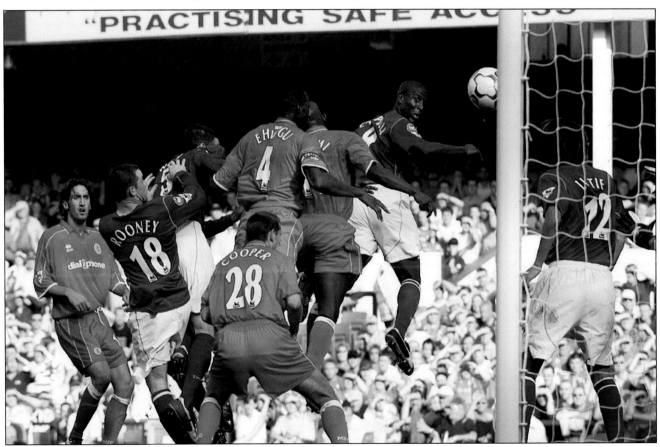

It had been a while since Kevin Campbell had scored two in a game so his brace against Middlesbrough in September 2002, sealing the first of the Blues' seven comebacks that season, was cause for celebration. He's pictured here glancing home his second of the afternoon.

There was many a memorable moment in the 2002-03 season and Tomasz Radzinski's last-minute winner against Southampton stood as proof that Wayne Rooney didn't have a monopoly on them. The unerring accuracy of his right-footed shot against the Saints left the majority of the ground open-mouthed as it seared into the top left-hand corner of the Gwladys Street net before they unashamedly danced the day away in celebration.

Steve Watson (partly hidden) scores his first goal of the game at the Reebok Stadium in January 2003.

Watson makes it 2-0 before half-time. The Blues went on to win 2-1 against struggling Bolton.

Relatively speaking there weren't that many in the Racecourse Ground to watch history being made, but those Evertonians who had made the short trip to Wrexham knew they'd been at the scene of something special. No sooner was he off the bench than 16-year-old Wayne Rooney was disrespectfully snatching away Tommy Lawton's long-standing record as the club's youngest-ever goalscorer. Minutes later he was finding the back of the net again.

It could have been the bedroom window of any Liverpool teenager. You wouldn't have known it belonged to English football and Everton's bright young hope Wayne Rooney. As the nation's press descended upon the Rooney family home in the city's Croxteth district it became clear that the young lad who stunned champions Arsenal with a curling last minute strike was just that – a boy who loved Everton.

It's difficult to decide which of Wayne Rooney's record-breaking goals was the more significant, his curling solo effort against champions Arsenal to become the Premiership's youngest-ever goalscorer or his individual winner at Leeds which put to bed a 51-year League hoodoo at Elland Road. Whatever the answer, there is no doubting that this picture, taken seconds after Wayne's goal against Leeds, is a beauty.

The pitch isn't big enough for the two of us! The future of English football unfolds before our very eyes in a telling scene at the end of the Anfield derby on December 22, 2003. With a quick glance, and a handshake, Wayne Rooney greets his opposite number Michael Owen. Just months earlier, Rooney had taken over Owen's record as the youngest player in the Premiership's history. Ironically the match itself finished goalless.

The less famous Wayne Rooney goal against Arsenal on location at Highbury in March 2003. Pascal Cygan backed off long enough to allow the teenager to squeeze a pinpoint shot into the bottom left-hand corner. It wasn't enough to guarantee the spoils that day but it was special in itself.

Sheer disbelief on a sea of faces as Wayne Rooney's first Premiership goal, against Arsenal, goes in off the bar. It's a perfect portrait of fan passion in the midst of battle.

You're my hero! The fan in Wayne Rooney comes out as he hoists Tomasz Radzinski into the air after the Canadian had scored another timely goal at Goodison.

He can do no wrong! David
Moyes acknowledges his
adoring fans.